THE LETTER

By IVAN BULLOCH

Written by Diane James
Photography by Toby Maudsley

CONTENTS

TWO-CAN

You do not need any special equipment to make or draw letters. In this book you will find out how to tear letters from coloured paper, how to stencil and print letters and even how to make letters using food!

Look at the shapes of letters in newspapers and magazines and collect the ones you like best.

A simple printing kit is useful for making invitations or your own writing paper, when you need more than one copy.

When you are cutting with a safety craft knife, always ask a grown-up for help.

paint

spray (for using with stencils)

printing kit

paint dish

flat brush

round brush

stencil brush

felt-tip pens

coloured paper

rubber

sponge

set square

pencils

italic pen

safety craft knife

ruler

All of the letters in the alphabet can be made from basic shapes such as circles, triangles, squares and rectangles. You can try this out for yourself by cutting shapes from coloured paper or using pre-cut shapes which you can buy in packets.

Most letters can be made using different combinations of shapes. See how many variations you can make of just one letter.

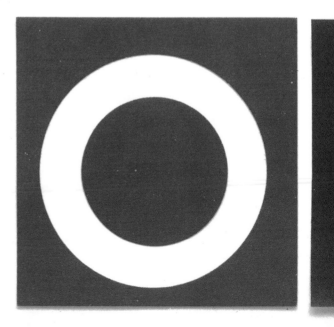

abcdef

ms
mi
vir

Letters do not have to be formed perfectly with neat edges and round curves! Try tearing letters from coloured paper so that they have a rough edge. You can also cut letters out without drawing them first. Cut or tear small pieces of coloured paper and use them to decorate your letters. When you have made a good collection, stick them on a piece of card to make a letter picture.

All of these letters were made from things you could probably find in your house.

We used building blocks, rope, straws, paper clips and modelling clay. Try to find other things that could be used and experiment with making letters that lie flat and letters that stand up!

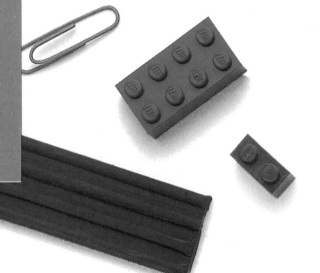

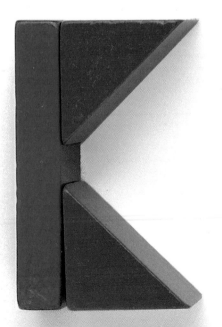

To make straw letters, cut
a small slit in the end of a
bendy straw so that it will
fit over another one. Cut
the straws to the lengths
you need.

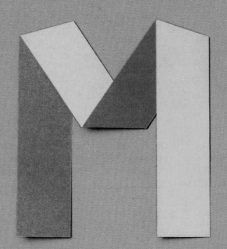

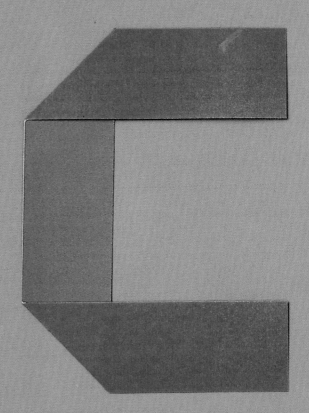

All of the letters here were made by folding a single strip of paper. Glue different coloured strips of paper together to begin with so that the folds will show up on your finished letters.

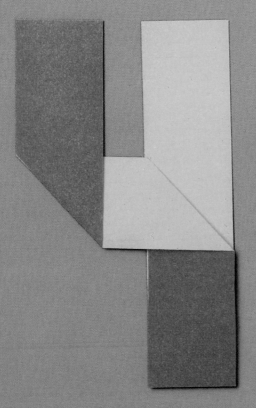

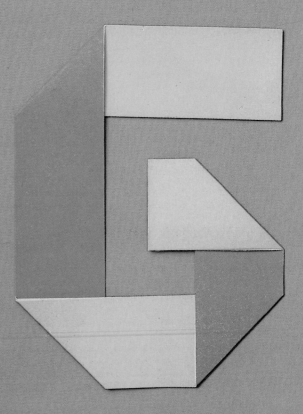

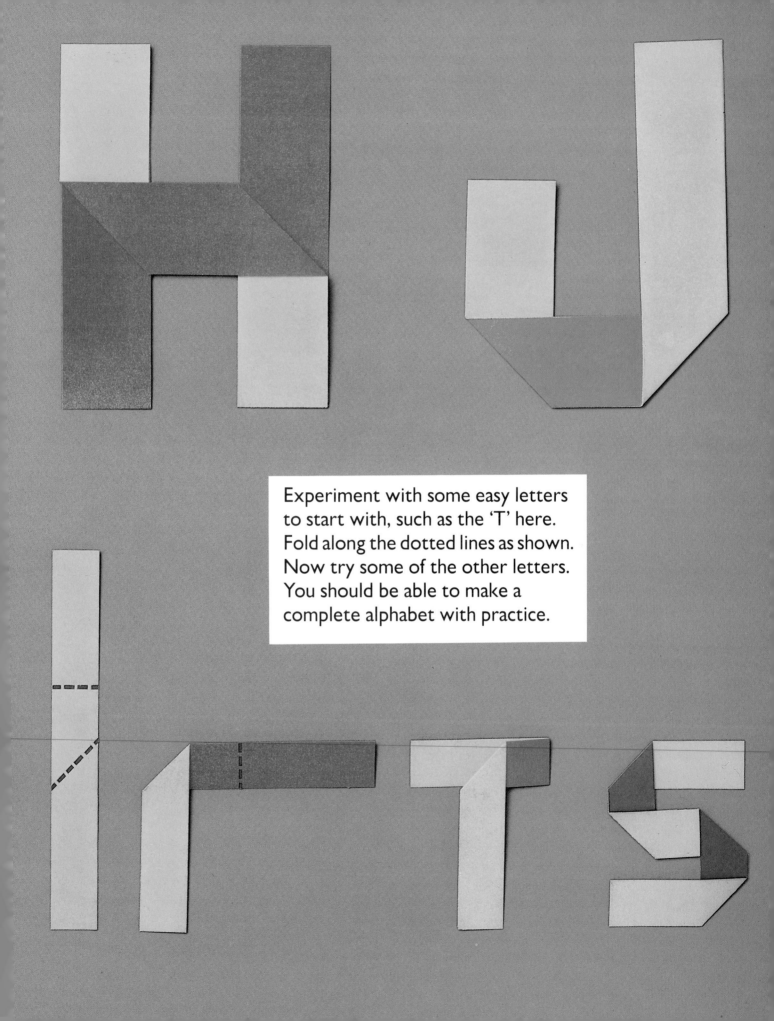

Experiment with some easy letters
to start with, such as the 'T' here.
Fold along the dotted lines as shown.
Now try some of the other letters.
You should be able to make a
complete alphabet with practice.

All of these letters have been made to stand up on their own. The cardboard and balsa wood letters slot together and the wooden letters at the bottom of the page are glued. Remember to make the slits exactly the same length so that they slot together neatly.

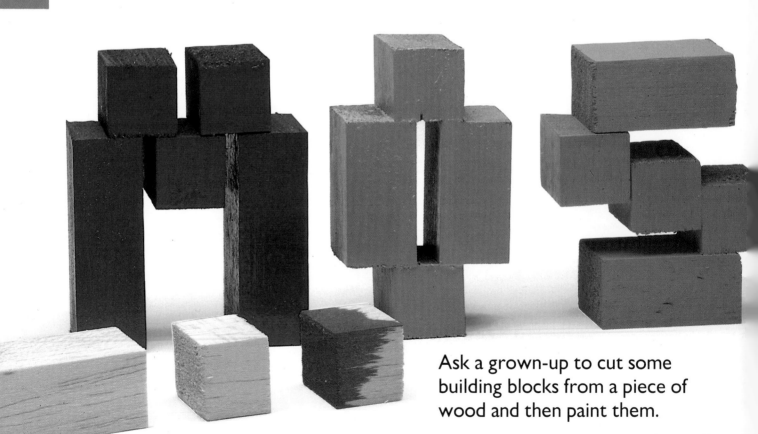

Ask a grown-up to cut some building blocks from a piece of wood and then paint them.

Try making a letter
sculpture like this one
using your initials.

Try making pop-up letters using folds and cuts to make them stand away from their background. Start with the pop-up 'A' below as an experiment. The solid lines are cutting lines and the dotted lines are fold lines. Score along the dotted lines with a scoring tool – or the back of a pair of scissors – to make them easier to fold.

Another method for making pop-up letters is simply to add a long tab to the top and bottom like the 'D' and the 'e' on the right. Fold a piece of card in half and glue the tabs on.

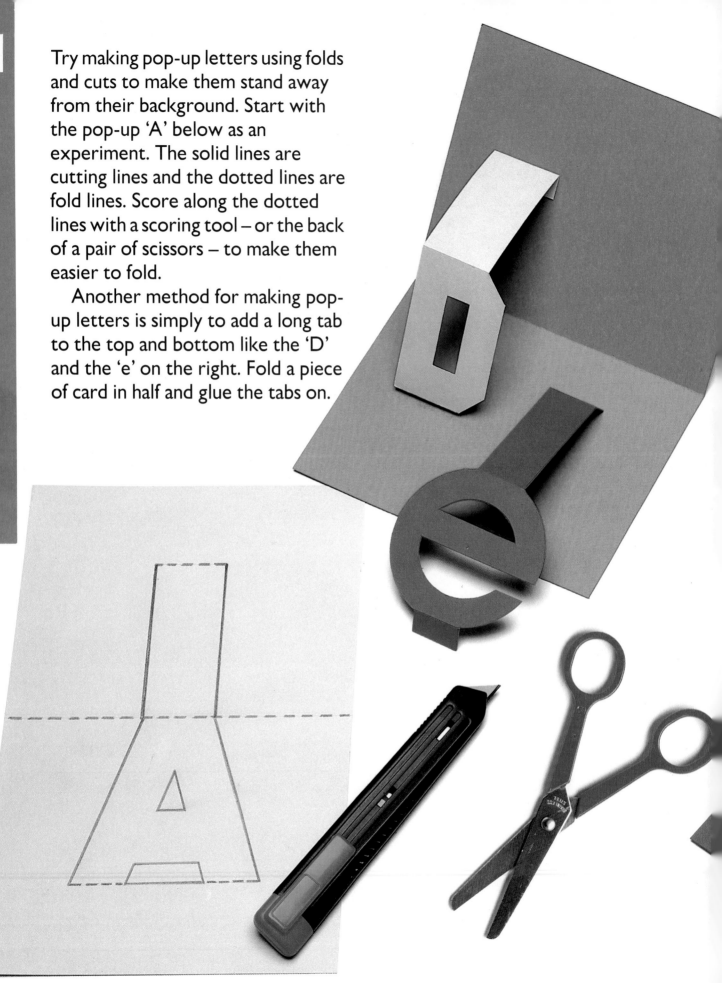

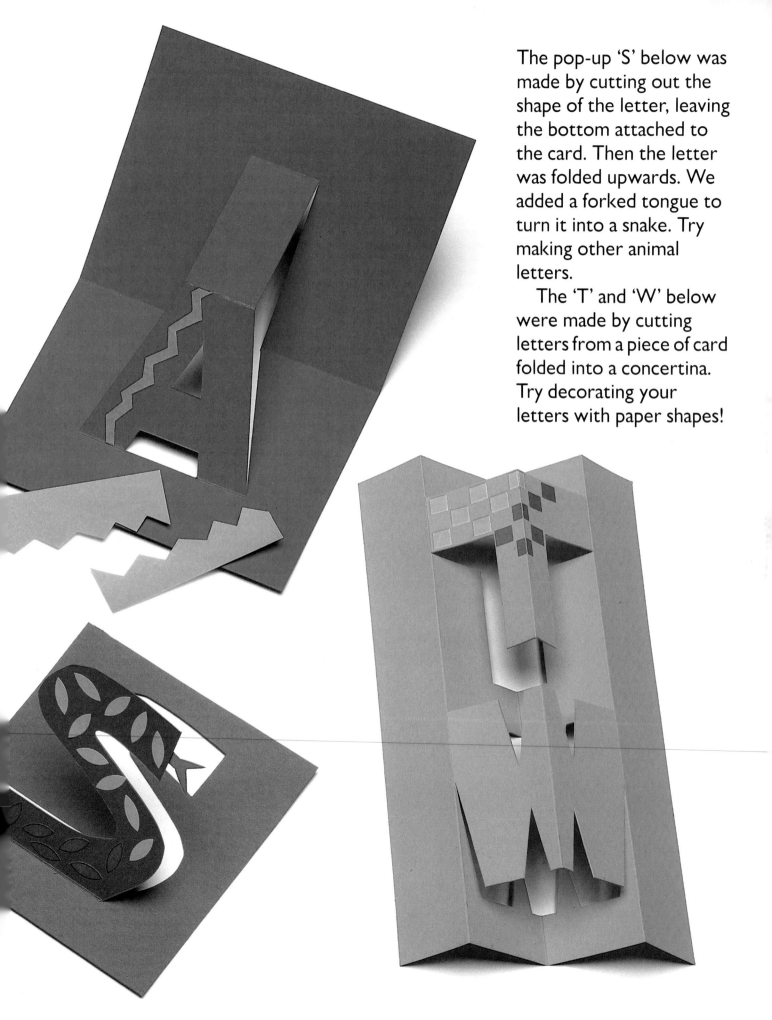

The pop-up 'S' below was made by cutting out the shape of the letter, leaving the bottom attached to the card. Then the letter was folded upwards. We added a forked tongue to turn it into a snake. Try making other animal letters.

The 'T' and 'W' below were made by cutting letters from a piece of card folded into a concertina. Try decorating your letters with paper shapes!

Printing and stencilling are good methods to use when you want to repeat letters more than once.

To make a potato print letter, ask a grown-up to cut a potato in half and help to cut the letter out of the potato so that it makes a raised surface to print from. Look for other objects, such as the rubbers here, which can be used to print from. Simple shapes are best!

You may need help to cut stencils but it is useful to have a complete alphabet! Use stencil card which is hard wearing and can be used over and over again. Keep the letters cut from the stencil card and try splattering paint over them, like the 'E' at the top of the page. Use an old toothbrush dipped in paint and rub it gently over your finger above the letter. You could also use a spray like the one on the equipment page. Use masking tape to keep your stencils in position without tearing the card.

Making patterns with letters is a good way to practise your printing and stencilling techniques and you can make some useful wrapping paper at the same time!

Try printing letters upside down and back to front to make interesting shapes. Or, try printing letters over other letters to make a new colour. The letter pattern in the bottom right was made by cutting letters from magazines and sticking them on to a piece of paper.

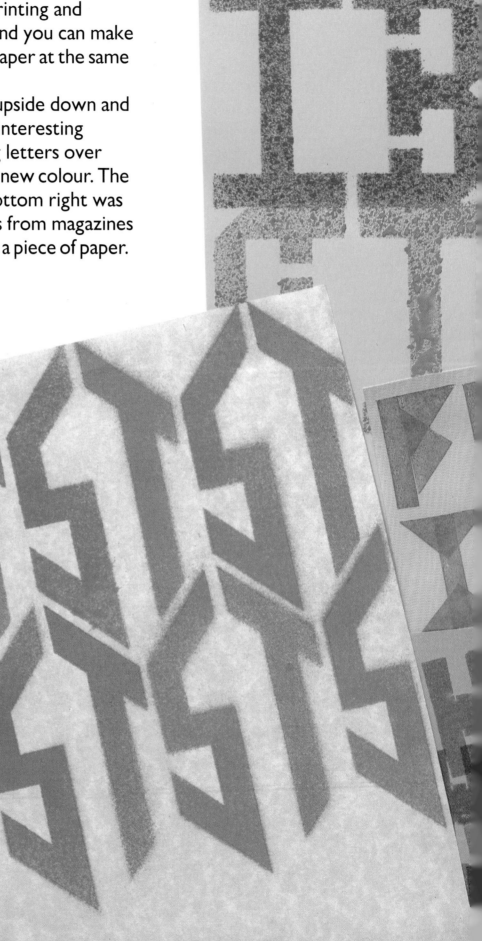

Here are some ideas for using letters to make bags, cards, badges, envelopes and writing paper. We used different techniques, such as printing, stencilling, cutting letters from coloured paper and making letters from paper shapes. Try making your own writing paper or postcards using one of these techniques for your name. You could add your address using a simple printing kit.

marié

52 KNOWSLEY

FC

52 KNOWSLEY

AVAV

li

20f MAGYAR POSTA

KÖZLEKEDÉSI MÚZEUM

fast POST PAR AVION

The next time you go out, look at the posters on walls and the carrier bags in shops. Try making your own! Find a plain carrier bag that you can stick letters on to, or make one by using an existing bag as a pattern. Put your name or initials on to your files and exercise books. Look at page 28 if you need inspiration for designing letter pictures!

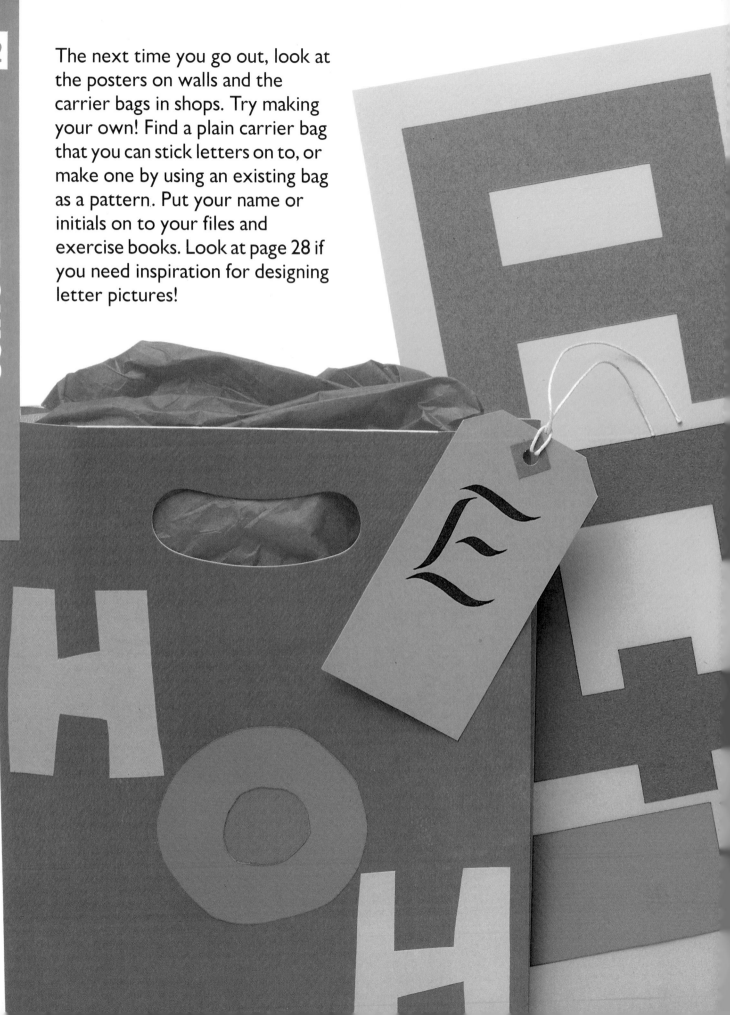

FOOD

You can make letters from nearly anything – including food! Look for brightly coloured sweets with interesting shapes. Some sweets and biscuits are already made into letters!

Ask a grown-up to make some icing and put it into an icing bag. Squeeze the icing bag gently and make letters on biscuits and cakes.

You could impress your friends at a party by making biscuits or cakes with their names on.

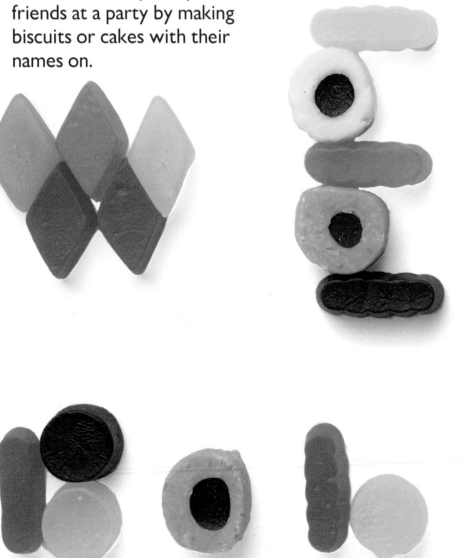

abcdefgh

All of these letters were made using an italic pen or a brush with a flat end. Practise making simple strokes first with an italic pen. Keep the nib at an angle of 45° so that it makes thick and thin lines. When you start writing letters, do not try to do a letter in one movement. Some letters need four or five strokes. Try using a brush with a flat end in the same way.

ivan paris

A

G H

It is hard to believe that these jolly characters were made entirely from letters and numbers! Start a collection of letters cut from newspapers and magazines. Look for large letters from headlines and posters. Try putting different letters together to make pictures.

When you are happy with the result, glue the letters on to paper or card. Or you could use letter pictures to decorate your exercise books.

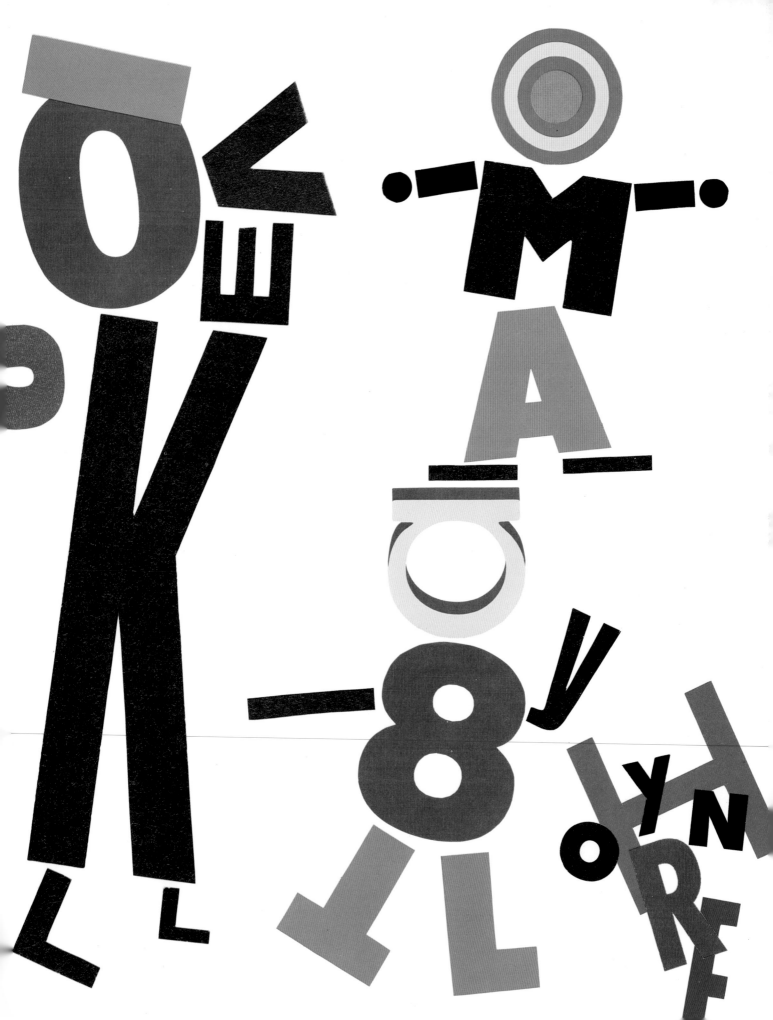

Here is an idea for making your summer T-shirts and baseball caps look really original!

Cut letters from brightly coloured felt. You can stick the letters on with fabric glue. Or, if you are good at sewing, stitch them on with cotton or wool using big stitches.

These T-shirts are for special occasions because you will have to take the letters off before you wash them!

You could also paint letters on to T-shirts using special fabric paints or pens.

Photograph of children by Fiona Pragoff